MARRIAGE BED DEFILED

James Stover

Written Words Publishing LLC
14189 E Dickinson Drive, Unit F
Aurora, Colorado 80014
www.writtenwordspublishing.com

Marriage Bed Defiled © 2021 by James Stover

All rights reserved. No part of this publication may be reproduced, stored in a retrieval system, or transmitted in any form by any means, electronic, mechanical, photocopying, recording, or otherwise, without the prior permission of the author.

Published by Written Words Publishing LLC 3/1/2021

ISBN: 978-1-7332357-8-5 (paperback)
ISBN: 978-1-7332357-9-2 (eBook)

Library of Congress Control Number: 2021903035

Cover Designed by Jayson Williams

Manufactured and printed in the United States of America

All Scripture quotations, unless otherwise indicated, are taken from the King James Version of the Bible, public domain. Scriptures noted as NKJV are taken from the New King James Version. Copyright © 1979, 1980, 1982 by Thomas Nelson, Inc. Used by permission. All rights reserved. Scriptures noted as NASB are taken from the New American Standard Bible, © 1960, 1962, 1963, 1968, 1971, 1972, 1973, 1975, 1977, 1995 by The Lockman Foundation. Used by permission. Scriptures noted as ESV are taken from The Holy Bible, English Standard Version®, Copyright © 2016 by Crossway Bibles, a division of Good News Publishers. Used by permission. All rights reserved. Scriptures noted as NIV are taken from the Holy Bible, New International Version® NIV®. Copyright © 1973, 1978, 1984, 2011 by the International Bible Society. Used by permission of Zondervan Publishing House. All rights reserved worldwide. Scriptures noted as RSV are taken from Revised Standard Version of the Bible, copyright © 1946, 1952, and 1971 National Council of the Churches of Christ in the United States of America. Used by permission. All rights reserved worldwide.

Table of Contents

Acknowledgements 1
Introduction 3
Chapter 1 The Aftermath 5
Chapter 2 My Story 9
Chapter 3 A Call to Action 13
Chapter 4 Marriage Vow 19
    I. Truth About Marriage, Divorce and Remarriage 21
    II. Establishing Truth 23
    III. The Order of God Is Out of Order 29
Chapter 5 Journey to Truth.. 33
    I. Law of Marriage 35
    II. Why Marriage?... 40
    III. Renewing the Mind... 43
Chapter 6 Prayer 49
    I. The Wills of God 51
Chapter 7 The Pauline Privilege..................................... 54
    I. Understanding Sin and the Law 63
    II. The Law of Separation 68
Chapter 8 Jezebel Spirit; Destroyer of Covenants.......... 76
Chapter 9 What About Me?... 79

ACKNOWLEDGEMENTS

I would like to take this time to thank some dear people to me, who were critical in my growth and spiritual development. When you know your purpose, you can look back on your life and see how the journey prepared you.

First, I would like to thank my parents. I remember moms purchasing $1,500 worth of encyclopedias (moms didn't have a lot of money either), and she would make me read and answer questions about what I read. This was molding me to do what I now love: research. I would like to thank both fathers; biological, who taught me how to maneuver the streets, critical to survival. Also, stepfather who taught me cleanliness and order. I would like to thank my sisters, brothers, aunts, uncles, cousins, and friends. "Thank you."

I would like to give a special thanks to Mrs. Marvel Clyburn and family. A truly remarkable woman who lives holiness, who guided me on the straight and narrow. A special thanks to my brothers in the faith: Tyrone Mclea, Corey Willis, Bishop Aurelio Givens-Little, and Abundant Life PPW, Camden, SC.

Thank you:

- John Stover - Yield Management
- Deuce King - Deuce King Publishing
  For inspiring to write
- Written Words Publishing LLC
  Publishing

- Jayson Williams - Upstate Images
  Cover Design

Finally, I would like to thank my daughters, Jayla, Imani, Aydin, and son, Sterling, who helped throughout the process. From critiquing rough drafts, helping with cover design and overall creativity. They are truly remarkable. Thank you for your service.

INTRODUCTION

As the morality of society steadily declines, we usher in new philosophies and beliefs. One subject in particular which is critical to any society's success is the family unit and God's intention through marriage. The marriage covenant has been trampled and turned into nothing but a mere contract where parties divorce and remarry for any and all disagreements, rather it's one or both.

Seventy percent (70%) of divorces today are instituted by women. This is the dilemma of the church today, sound doctrine. The women were to teach the children and raise the young girls to be women and love their husbands. Now, the roles have drastically changed as there is an agenda to de-masculate men. Women are taught to be independent. Even when she needs help from the government, a man cannot be present. Men are married to their careers and hobbies and motivated by money over family time.

This book is designed to hopefully dispel the myths and lies about God's marriage covenant. Prayerfully, open blinded eyes through the truth of God's word. I penned this book as a testament to a superior being and creator. Every day, we go through life programmed but failed to stop for a second and ask why. Why do we do the things we do? Why do we bother to get married especially? Even though I came through a very toxic, lesson learning marriage of 18 years, it was the empathy seeing others go through the same similar fate. The pain that one suffers is why divorce is considered violent (an act of ripping apart). The disappointment and fear the children of failing marriages have to endure, not to exclude staying in some marriages, would be detrimental to the child's psychology also. Still, it goes back to the route. Why do we do it and why are so many failing at a tremendous rate?

CHAPTER 1

THE AFTERMATH

Marriages, as well as all relationships, can seem very complicated. There are many factors to include that contribute to the human behavior of any particular being. These factors can include one's character, morals, values, and upbringing. Also, along with one's spirituality, mental health and overall miseducation on this important covenant.

I decided to tackle this task as marriages are failing miserably. Being married for 18 years (mostly toxic), I began to see I was not alone. I couldn't go anywhere without people talking about relationship problems—work, TV, friends, social media, etc. You name it, there it was that dreadful topic and the pain some people were suffering from failed marriages and that nail in the coffin, "divorce."

I made a conscious decision to not harp on my broken marriage, but use my God given purpose to expose the lies and myths on marriage, even though my broken marriage was painful. I will from time to time in this book reflect on my marriage to give the reader an idea of what I've been through and how I got here. I embrace it as the ultimate learning experience. It ignites a fire to learn more and turn this vicious cycle of broken families into thriving, whole, complete family units which in turn makes a society stronger and ethically better.

Trust me, I have been emotionally drained, manipulated, cheated on, lied to, and faced that evil spirit of narcissism (all mental health is demonic to me because your mind is under attack and not whole). I have one simple formula: whatever is manifested in the physical, was birthed or planted in the spiritual. So, whatever is running rampant on the earth, started in the spiritual. I will go in depth on this subject later in the book.

Here is a little insight into my story. Like I previously stated, I have been married for 18 years; three beautiful daughters as a result (smile). When I met my soon to be wife, it was around 2001 and I was a year removed from another failed relationship. My wife was a church going person, sung in the choir; I mean every Sunday she was going to church. That was so attractive to me as I was going through my own spiritual renaissance. I heard from the Lord clearly that "a lot of people think they are worshipping Me but they're not." That illuminated that scripture in Matthew 7:23 (KJV), *"And then will I profess unto them, I never knew you: depart from me, ye that work iniquity."* This scripture stuck with me. If these people were doing things in the name of our savior, why did He reject them? Why was God giving me visions of wolves or wild dogs tearing at my flesh? Why did God tell me you are sleeping with the enemy? Finally, why did God tell me He is going to put me behind enemy lines? At that time, little did I know, I would be learning and experiencing the answer to these questions in my own marriage.

In my marriage, I was grossly uneducated and very naive. I ignored all the warning signs of character. I now consider myself a spiritual disciple who is not by my own righteousness, but the righteousness of God. He has revealed His mysteries to those that have an ear to hear and eyes to see.

I wasn't a church going person, yet I marveled at the ignorance of the current church goer as many did not know the Bible or desire to know. I really got into church a couple of years before my wife and I met. I went all in. Right or wrong, the church hurt more than it helped. I am not playing victim as I did some things that contributed to the demise of my marriage. I idolized my wife and I would go to hell for her. I believe this is what Adam went through for the Bible says the woman was deceived! (Timothy 2:14) I believe Adam loved her so much he sinned. I couldn't understand why people portray to be something they are not. I didn't provide a stable in the word spiritual covering, so it was a constant spiritual struggle. This is in no way an excuse for someone else's actions as some people go to church all their life and don't live an ounce of it. That's insanity, retardation (slow in learning). I will not get into specifics about my marriage as that would be distasteful, only to use as a teaching tool. Trust me, I learned a lot.

To even begin we will have to peel back layers like an orange to get to the juice of the matter. We will conclude that there is a supreme being; a creator of the universe and mankind in general. For the sake of time and confusion, I will not use this platform to debate evolution or any other ideology that tries to dismiss an architect of creation. So, with that being said, we will look at the divine order of man. Why the marriage covenant? The purpose of marriage and how is the relationship of an earthly marriage compared to a spiritual walk with your Father, the creator.

Once we better understand the covenant of marriage:

1) We will understand the purpose of marriage.
2) We will learn the proper conduct in marriage.

3) We will understand the laws and boundaries in marriage.
4) We will be better equipped to recognize and defeat physical as well as spiritual attacks on marriage.
5) Finally, God is no respecter of person (Acts 10:34). God has a Divine order. Man, woman and child have an important position to play.

LET US PRAY FOR EYES TO SEE AND EARS TO HEAR!

CHAPTER 2

MY STORY

It all began as I was pursuing my calling God gave me to change. "A lot of people think they're worshipping me, but they're not."

Then I began to dwell on the scripture, Matthew 7:21-23 (NASB), *"Not everyone who says to Me, 'Lord, Lord,' will enter the kingdom of heaven, but the one who does the will of My Father who is in heaven will enter. Many will say to Me on that day, 'Lord, Lord, did we not prophesy in Your name, and in Your name cast out demons, and in Your name perform many miracles?' And then I will declare to them, 'I never knew you; leave Me, you who practice lawlessness.'"*

I ask myself, why did God say this if they were doing these things in His name? Does God show up at times just to defend His name? Does God still use enemies for His purpose? So, I looked at the charge God gave me. "A lot of people think they are worshipping Me but they are not, and through the information you love to obtain I will expose the lies of the devil."

The word worship—we have to worship God in spirit and truth (John 4:23-24). At this time, God was waking me up at odd hours of the morning and all I could do was study and write. Sometimes 3, 4 o'clock in the morning. This was my worship with God as He continued to reveal things to me and teach me His word. True worship is getting intimate with God like being intimate with your wife behind closed doors, under the covers. It isn't for show, as no one sees you, but out of true devotion and love. "True worship comes from a person who is deeply emotional and who loves deep and sound doctrine."

It's like the gift of sex, which is supposed to be reserved for marriage. However, like many things God intended for good have been perverted and diluted by man. Notice I said man and not the devil, because he can only entice you with the desires already in you (James 1:14). Sometimes, we give Satan too much credit when he's already defeated. Man has trampled over this since the beginning of time and has grown worse. Sex is nothing more than lust now; it has gone from a gift to a burden. Babies born out of wedlock, broken homes, infidelity—women have gone from virtuous to whores. God has turned men and women over to the unnatural affection of men having sex with men and women having sex with women. This is just the results of the physical, but everything starts in the spiritual. So, if we have adultery and fornication here on earth, there has to be spiritual adultery and fornication which God clearly forbids in the first commandment. The spiritual fornication that is being committed time and time again is the acceptance of false doctrine. This isn't to attack no-one person(s), but exposing truth, as Acts 17:30 (ESV) says, *"The times of ignorance God overlooked, but now he commands all people everywhere to repent."* Hosea 4:6 (ESV), *"My people are destroyed for lack of knowledge; because you have rejected knowledge, I reject you..."*

There is coming a time when God will not overlook our ignorance and we are ignorant because we reject knowledge (intimate relationship) which therefore is destroying us as a people. To reject God is to reject knowledge of Him, the root word of knowledge is the word know. In its past tense, the word is 'knew.' Anytime a couple was intimate in the book of scriptures, it was characterized by the word 'knew.'

"...Adam knew Eve his wife, and she conceived..." (Genesis 4:1 ESV).

To know God is to become intimate with Him. We enter into a covenant with God. If marriages are supposed to be our physical representation of our spiritual connection to an all Supreme Being, then is it safe to say, with the state of marriages today, something is terribly wrong? I wasn't brought up in the church to learn all the protocol and traditions, so it wasn't that hard to unlearn false doctrine. Let's just keep it real. Most people don't even read their Bible let alone study it. If they do read, how many have trouble understanding it?

The church to me should be the most powerful and leading institution in the world but the churches are not leading. They are following the ways of the world and its philosophies have crept in and took strongholds in the minds of individuals. Church has become a place of performance from the old-time grunting, yelling preachers with the organs playing (and they're really not saying anything) to the elaborate singing and dancing which often times is the same dance and beat we heard and saw in the world. The church has fallen from a place of power where people are truly being transformed, taught and being prepared to be accepted in God's Divine family. Preachers have become more consumed with money, flaunting wealth, worldly accomplishments, and degrees. Now do not take this the wrong way. Schooling is good and has its proper place in the church. As I say all the time, math and science is its own universal language.

If Satan is the God of this world (2 Corinthians 4:4), we can believe he has influence in this world (Daniel 3). The phrase "God of this world" indicates that Satan is the major influence or spirit that is manifested in the physical on the ideals, opinions, goals, and views of the majority of people. His influence has dominated the world's financial, education and religious systems which in turn has shaped the minds, behavioral patterns and beliefs of many. Now we can see how an Adolf Hitler rose to power and deceived many—the power of influence.

When it comes to the divine things of the kingdom, it takes a divine God to call and teach a man (preacher) to understand and break down spiritual things. This is seen when the Apostle John was on the island of Patmos and the angel appeared to him, "Here, John. Take the book." John was instructed to eat and digest the book, meaning:

Take the book: meaning John really didn't want it.
Eat and digest: meaning consume the book, get it on the inside and break it down. *God was instructing John on the things of God.

When we look at the many religions of the world, it's like a smorgasbord. Are we supposed to just choose one? That's utterly confusing and we know who the author of confusion is. When we study and read scripture with understanding, we can see that God's religion is Holiness which is a lifestyle.

"Speak to all the congregation of the people of Israel and say to them, **You shall be holy***, for I the* **Lord your God am holy***."* (Leviticus 19:2 ESV).

Chapter 3

A Call to Action

This is why I have to dedicate my time, pain and suffering too. It is somewhat self-therapeutic. As I help others, it helps me deal with the pain, agony and misery of adultery and broken marriages. At the time of writing this, I have encountered many men and women going through the similar trails of lies, deceit and cheating. Men in particular, as I am a man, and being in men circles. I feel their pain, their hurt, their disappointment.

While diving into this journey, God has revealed and taken me down many roads. It is definitely an attack on His holy covenant. He has opened my eyes to the stepfather and makeshift family's dilemma, to the whole homosexual agenda.

Everything is being perverted and putting a stain on his glory. Every fire needs a source. Can the broken relationships of God's natural intentions, a man and a woman, be fueling the unnatural relations of a man and a man or woman and a woman? As many have been hurt beyond repair in their natural relationship, this is the homosexual epidemic as people just want to be loved; loved without the hurt.

Satan is wise and cunning just like the Bible says.

Keeping in context of my God-given purpose of exposing his lies, I will be undertaking a spiritual battle of the ages. I will have to be in constant prayer. I will have to become a watchman to remain pure; purity as power. The Bible declares the prayers of a "righteous," untainted, pure man availeth much. "The effectual fervent." (James 5:16)

I even find myself being somewhat of a marriage vigilant when I see men, especially those who I know are married, drool over half naked or tight-fitting clothed women. I sigh and give them that energy and look at them like "Aren't you married?" It's a good but sometimes strange feeling. Many times, I feel like an alien from another planet. I guess this is what the Bible means when it says that we are in this world but not of it.

Six months into my marital breakdown (emotional detachment makes it longer than that), it's been an up and down emotional rollercoaster. In this time of turmoil, I made the conscious decision to see what my creator wanted and expected of me. I have been befriended by some real followers of Christ who eat, breathe and sleep the Messiah.

To be followers, it meant more than just learning about Christ but applying what you learned to everyday life. The spirit realm is real. How can it not be if God is spirit and He commands us to worship in spirit and truth? The scripture tells us that our war is not with flesh and blood, ex. the physical person, but in the spirit realm (Ephesians 6:12). The spirit is that which is behind personal behavioral actions. These brothers knew I was in for a spiritual battle as Satan has declared war on God's Holy covenant. Those that are caught up in adultery, lying, cheating, and manipulating are trampling all over God's covenant.

Physical, emotional and mental abuse are all contrary to God's way. I have been guilty of verbal abuse with some instances turning physical which I am deeply sorry for and had to repent. No matter the severity of the offenses, there is no excuse for neither. The sad part is how Satan (influence) blinds one from seeing their part in the destruction of a marriage. You might even go through times where you won't be able to talk to your children, false attempts to get restraining orders, threats; "If you don't do that, imma do this."

So, you just have to stand in boldness of God's protection and favor and remain pure. The more a person hardens their heart to God's word (truth) they open themself up to portals for more satanic influence and in the process become desensitized to sin. People like this are not even challenged in the modern churches let alone sin being preached and the consequences of it. People in sinful lifestyles have become common in the church and carry on functions in the church from Pastor, choir member, musicians, and members.

ACTION STATEMENT:

> You learn to gain knowledge. Once you know better, you can do better. I drew a line in the sand to follow God's word. It's been awhile out of the presence of my wife and, honestly, I still feel a type of way about the defilement. However, I choose to trust God and in return love me.

Many Christians believe God wants us to be happy. That's a true statement, however, our happiness shouldn't come at the expense of doing what's contrary to God's word. People twist ideology in theology to say divorce is right. It's okay to be with someone else when the one you made a vow before God leaves; surely you deserve to be happy.

I remember sitting in a church. They had a tradition called showers of scriptures where people in the congregation would stand and recite their favorite scripture. I saw one problem with this: isn't this useless if the scripture they're reciting, they have no understanding of it? If you have no understanding, how can you rightly divide what to believe?

It reminds me of a movie I watched when I was younger. It was about vampires which we could say symbolize evil. We know vampires are supposed to be frightened of crosses and in this particular scene the man held up a cross, but it had no effect on the vampire as he crumbled the cross in his hand. I watched in bewilderment and shock as in all movies the cross worked. Even though it's Hollywood and it was just a movie, there was some truth behind it. In the following scene, the vampire says something I would never forget: "How do you expect this to work when you don't believe?" Many people recite scripture and don't even understand the scripture. It can lead to believing misinterpretations which is ultimately a lie. Some people say, "Surely God would want you to divorce and remarry when your spouse is alive. He doesn't want us to suffer..."

Was it too much for the Messiah to suffer for mankind, to die a brutal death? He suffered for the remission of man's sin. One that was found blameless to be beaten, spit upon and his side pierced with a spear. When the Bible says, "pick up your cross," this is one of those scriptures we sadly don't understand.

It all began for me as I was pursuing my purpose and calling from God. A scripture was illuminated in my mind. Matthew 7:21-23 (NASB) was the scripture I dwelled on. *"Not everyone who says to Me, 'Lord, Lord,' will enter the kingdom of heaven, but the one who does the will of My Father who is in heaven will enter. Many will say to Me on that day, 'Lord, Lord, did we not prophesy in Your name, and in Your name cast out demons, and in Your name perform many miracles?' And then I will declare to them. 'I never knew you; leave Me, you who practice lawlessness."*

I asked myself, why did God say this if they were doing these things in His name? So, I looked at my purpose and the charge God has given me which simply says: <u>A lot of people think they're worshiping me but they're not and through the information you love to obtain through research, I will expose the lies of the devil.</u>

True worship is worshipping God in spirit and in truth (John 4:23-24). At this time, God was waking me up at all hours of the morning and all I can do is study and write; sometimes 3, 4 o'clock in the morning. This was my worship with God as He continued to reveal things to me and teach me His word. True worship is getting intimate with God like being intimate with your wife behind closed doors under the covers. It isn't for show as no one sees you but out of true devotion and love. True worship comes from a person who is deeply invested and who loves sound doctrine. It's like the gift of sex which is supposed to be reserved for marriage.

However, like many things God intended for good and for specific purposes have been perverted and diluted by man. Notice I said man and not Satan because Satan can only entice you with the desires already in you (James 1:14). Sometimes, we give Satan too much credit when he's already defeated. Man has trampled over God's covenant since the beginning of time and it has grown worse. Sex is nothing more than lust now. It has gone from a gift to a burden. Babies born out of wedlock or even aborted, broken homes and infidelity. Women have gone from virtuous to whores. Men have gone from Kings to Ahabs (see Jezebel).

And both men and women have succumbed to the unnatural affection of the same sex. This is just the results in the physical, but everything starts in the spiritual. So, there has to be spiritual immorality which begins with a mindset, moral compass and understanding of scripture.

Chapter 4

Marriage Vow

"I, ___, take you, ___, to be my wedded husband/wife, to have and to hold, from this day forward, for better, for worse, for richer, for poorer, in sickness and in health, to love and to cherish, (man-worship; women-obey), till death do us part, according to God's holy law, in the presence of God I make this vow."

What is a vow? A solemn promise, oath, pledge, bond, or commitment.

I take you, meaning I choose you. Many people think of love as a feeling or just simply an emotion. Love is an expression of God's gift to every human being; the free will to choose. With that free will choice, we choose who we want to marry and give our feelings and emotions to. God commands us to love everyone and that cannot be based just on a feeling. To love some people, we must first be willing to forgive, thus we see love as forgiveness and both are a choice.

Love is also God and God is truth. To love God is to love truth. We know that God is pure, God is the truth, God is forgiving, God is long suffering, and everywhere I put God you can replace with love. Choosing to love somebody is to love them in the context of God's standard, for that is true love. That is why the Bible says, *"Husbands, love your wives, just as Christ also loved the church…"* (Ephesians 5:25 NKJV).

Now, the next couple of lines are really self-explanatory. "For better or worse, for richer or poor, in sickness and health, to love and to cherish." Now, a man is to worship. We know, to worship God, it has to be in spirit and truth. So, can we say a man is to stay spiritually connected to God and hold to His truth, not opinions or worldly values? As long as a man does this, the woman should obey; not as a slave, but submit to her husband under the order of God to be a helpmate and strive to be a virtuous woman, not a woe-man.

Now, here is the part that I think society takes for granted, and **like the Pharisees in Moses' time,** we're looking to divorce for any reason. Till death do us part, according to God's holy law, marriage is God's holy covenant. But just like the job of Satan, he comes to pervert the things of God.

The marriage covenant is turned into a marriage contract. There is a difference between a covenant and a contract. A contract is a legal document that can be annulled by any one person if the other party refuses to live up to the agreement. **A covenant is a spiritual agreement or promise. It is a perpetual promise which means never ending or changing.** So, just from these simple definitions, we see marriage has been distorted from the holy covenant, a perpetual promise by both parties to uphold a promise before God until death does us part, even if one party breaks his promise. To a contract, "I will remain married until you do something." So that asks another question: Is divorce and remarriage biblical as long as your covenant spouse is still living?

"Till death do us part," something we can touch on later. However, if marriage is viewed as God's holy covenant, where a covenant is a never ending or forever promise you vowed to fulfill no matter what, then we can draw our conclusion.

I. Truth About Marriage, Divorce and Remarriage

Where is God? Why do we as followers have to be viewed as weak? Why doesn't God stand up for those who follow His ways and are done dirty, wrongly accused, and persecuted? Is this why some people fall from the faith, because they view God as a weak God? When we become peacemakers or the forgivers, why doesn't my life feel blessed? **It seems the worldly just shake it off, have the most fun and continue to prosper. Or is the madness making me become self-righteous**? For he who has no sin cast the first stone. What may seem happy on the outside may well be dark and lost on the inside. When the anger subsides, it always comes full circle to true. God is not mocked. You reap what you sow.

What does the Bible truly say about marriage, divorce and remarriage?

Many Christians, the fake and well-meaning ones, are caught up in divorce and remarriage. They either stick to their traditions or what they have been taught in church, whether right or wrong. The question is this: Do we really seek (study to show ourselves approved) to see what God's word says? Let's examine what the word says.

As I previously stated in the marriage vows:

1. **It is a vow; a holy vow unto God**
2. **It states in sickness and in health**

3. Till death do us part

If marriage is a holy vow, we must understand what holy is. Holy is to be consecrated and set apart for God's use. Leviticus 10:10 says to make a distinction between the clean and the unclean. So, a marriage based on the biblical principles of God's word should be totally different from the world's view, where God is equal to truth or being true. So, if marriage is to be different as even James 4:4 (ESV) states, *"You adulterous people! Do you not know that friendship with the world is enmity with God? Therefore whoever wishes to be a friend of the world makes himself an enemy of God."*

Now, let us understand that the law of marriage is for the saved as well as the unsaved, much like the law of gravity. However, we cannot surely expect an unsaved (lover of the world, enemy of God) person to conduct their marriage like a saved (worshipping in spirit and truth) person. Thus, you have divorce. Divorce is not of the spirit, but the flesh, i.e., a feeling, selfishness and unforgiveness. We can see that a holy marriage covenant is based on truth and God's wisdom laid out in his laws. Romans 7:1 (KJV) says, *"...brethren, (for I speak to them that know the law,) how that the law hath dominion over a man as long as he liveth?"* I will get back to this.

Back to James 4:4. Notice how God calls a person who is friends with the world an adulteress, which is for the man. This is spiritual adultery. I am a firm believer that what is birthed or manifested in the physical is first impregnated or planted in the spiritual. Being a lover of the world, it's ways, it's false doctrine, tradition of men, and not cultivating or setting yourself apart to be holy and used by

God creates a seed. Sometime in the future this seed will manifest into unhealthy soul ties and full-blown adultery.

Now back to the law of marriage, or what the Bible commands about marriage. But before I go there I just want to make a statement. When I'm purchasing something from the store and I'm having trouble trying to figure out how it operates, I refer to the owner's manual. Who better to know what's wrong than the people who made it? If we so-called Christians believe God is our creator, then why don't we refer to the owner's manual concerning our lives called in the Bible?

Roman 7:2-3 (NIV) says, *"For example, by law a married woman is bound to her husband as long as he is alive, but if her husband dies, she is released from the law that binds her to him. So then, if she has sexual relations with another man while her husband is still alive, she is called an adulteress. But if her husband dies, she is released from that law and is not an adulteress if she marries another man."*

II. Establishing Truth

Most historians begin with the unsubstantiated notion that primitive people slowly developed civilizations from rudimentary beginnings. When instead archaeology around the world revealed advanced ancient technology without discernible periods of evolution. This appearance of cultures processing advanced technology approximately 4,000 years ago is consistent with the flood, the proliferation of intelligent people on the plains of shunts and their subsequent scattering from the Tower of Babel.

The Septuagint, a Greek version of the Hebrew Bible (or Old Testament), including the Apochapra, made for

Greek-speaking Jews in Egypt in the 3rd and 2nd centuries BC and adopted by the early Christian churches. This is one of the oldest manuscripts that date past European Colonization. Some say the manuscripts of the holy scriptures are a plagiarism of the ancient Egyptian religion, Kemet. I am no historian, so I will just keep it basic. I am not here to argue timelines and do an in-depth research of ancient religions. I am just noting the striking resemblance these religions have. Even in the concept of pyramid building during the 25th dynasty, the old kingdom of Egypt. We see parallelism to stories being told. The pyramids were designed to serve as a gigantic stairway by which the soul of a deceased pharaoh could ascend to heavens. Could it be possible that we see this story in Genesis 11:1-9? Man became a united race generations following the Great Flood. Speaking a single language and migrating westward comes to the land of Shinar (a general region in Mesopotamia). They agree (one accord) to build a city and a tower to reach heaven.

The moral of the story is that they (the people) continued to deny or be in defiance to a command. God let them continue to build (go their way; oppose command; sin) so that there could be a historical record for all future generations. The story of Genesis continues that God had to step in and confuse their language and scattered them across the Earth. Why? Keeping in order with respect to history, the ancient Egyptian civilizations were advanced, not just some primitive people. They had mathematics, astrology, science, etc.

In their advanced technology and way of thinking, God saw that if these people came together on one accord, it's nothing that they couldn't do (Genesis 11:4-9). Even though the people were unified, it was for the wrong reasons. God had to confuse the languages to slow down the increased wickedness that comes with advanced knowledge. We see evidence of great structures in the building of the pyramids.

Like I said, I'm not here to debate religion (I do not believe the creator created most of, if any of these modern religions). I am simply trying to present an argument that the creator had a moral code of morality that is perpetual and a law of the universe.

What do I mean? Well, let's look at the law of gravity. This is a universal law, where there is gravity, things just don't float into space. The law of gravity is for everyone, as everyone is susceptible to it for it is the law. How about the law of conception? That every human being had to be birthed through the womb of a woman. As we see in the examples, these are laws and principles that provide the balance, order, and conduct of human beings and the universe. Laws are simply instructions on how one is to conduct himself in harmony with the universe and society.

So, with that being said, let's apply this to marriage. If marriage is a divine institution of a holy God, then it has to be governed by God's holy law. Religion is one of the most debatable topics of all time. It has been here from ancestor to ancestor. It has been the most misunderstood, manipulated and ostracized cultural staple in the history of mankind. Once again, I'm not here to debate religions. I can only relate to mine. However, once again I do want to intentionally present it from a different point of view. That is to show that human beings have been created by a superior being with a moral code. These moral codes are laws or instructions on how an individual should conduct themselves in harmony with the universe.

We, as humans, rebel by nature. We sometimes wrongly look at laws as restricting freedom. If I was walking down the beach and I saw a sign that read, "Danger. No swimming. Sharks in the area," am I going to get rebellious? Will I feel as though they're restricting my freedom, or will I heed the warning and steer myself of possible danger? This is the same concept of God's laws. They are here for us to live by, to protect us.

If marriage is defined as a holy institution of God, then who is better to instruct on the conduct of marriage? Who better to define the participation of marriage and the role of each involved? The teaching has to take place in the church as it is a divine institution. Not our schools, government or worldly leaders. As we can see by the divorce rate and laws passed to broaden the participants of marriage, the church has failed. The church has become I.L.L.—illiterate, lazy and lethargic.

This is a comparison between ancient Egyptian laws of conduct as opposed to the book of scriptures.

42 laws of Kemet

1. I have not committed sin.
2. I have not committed robbery with violence.
3. I have not stolen.
4. I have not slain men or women.
5. I have not stolen food.
6. I have not swindled offerings.
7. I have not stolen from God/Goddess.
8. I have not told lies.
9. I have not carried away food.
10. I have not cursed.
11. I have not closed my ears to truth.
12. I have not committed adultery.

13. I have not made anyone cry.
14. I have not felt sorrow without reason.
15. I have not assaulted anyone.
16. I am not deceitful.
17. I have not stolen anyone's land.
18. I have not been an eavesdropper.
19. I have not falsely accused anyone.
20. I have not been angry without reason.
21. I have not seduced anyone's wife.
22. I have not polluted myself.
23. I have not terrorized anyone.
24. I have not disobeyed the Law.
25. I have not been exclusively angry.
26. I have not cursed God/Goddess.
27. I have not behaved with violence.
28. I have not caused disruption of peace.
29. I have not acted hastily or without thought.
30. I have not overstepped my boundaries of concern.
31. I have not exaggerated my words when speaking.
32. I have not worked evil.
33. I have not used evil thoughts, words or deeds.
34. I have not polluted the water.
35. I have not spoken angrily or arrogantly.
36. I have not cursed anyone in thought, word or deeds.
37. I have not placed myself on a pedestal.
38. I have not stolen what belongs to God/Goddess.
39. I have not stolen from or disrespected the deceased.
40. I have not taken food from a child.
41. I have not acted with insolence.
42. I have not destroyed property belonging to God/Goddess.

10 Commandments

1. You shall have no other gods before Me.
2. You shall make no idols.
3. You shall not take the name of the Lord your God in vain.
4. Keep the Sabbath day holy.
5. Honor your father and your mother.
6. You shall not murder.
7. You shall not commit adultery.
8. You shall not steal.
9. You shall not bear false witness against your neighbor.
10. You shall not covet.

Documentation - hand copied documents called the manuscripts provide proof of New and Old Testament historical consistency.

Archeological findings - excavation sites and artifacts provide evidence that many of the people and places mentioned in the Bible really existed.

Jesus (Messiah) - was a true historical person documented by the Apostles and early Jewish manuscripts. The early Roman leaders and historians wrote about the Messiah.

Fulfilled prophecies - the Bible contains many prophecies that have been fulfilled including detailed descriptions of events.

Redeemed lives - the Bible speaks to the (heart) condition of the human soul in a way that it has a life changing impact on individuals from all beliefs and cultures.

*Paul once was a murderer of Christians.

Although the Bible was written over many centuries by different writers, the message remains coherent and consistent.

More scientific proof is seen in Genesis 2:7 (KJV), *"And the Lord God formed man of the dust of the ground, and breathed into his nostrils the breath of life; and man became a living soul."*

Some allege that the creation of Adam is non-scientific and a bunch of fables. As the scripture says, God created man from the dust of the earth. However, there are scientific proofs that can make the creation story make sense. The human body is made up of materials and minerals found on the surface of the ground. There are 59 elements found in the human body and all are found on the earth's crust. Oxygen, being the most abundant element on the earth crust, makes up 65% of the human body. Carbon is also abundant which makes up 18% and hydrogen is 10%. So, again as we see, the Bible says perfectly what the scientific composition of the human body is (clay = h20 + earth's crust). As seen in the equation, the human body is not just made up of dust, but water to form clay.

"Remember, I beseech thee, that thou hast made me as the clay; and wilt thou bring me into dust again?" (Job 10:9 KJV).

God breathed life into these clay bodies giving them a soul.

III. The Order of God Is Out of Order

Position or the order of God for the man/woman, the God family.

God made man in His image (Genesis 1:20,27) and characteristics, and never identified Himself as a female

God and gave men dominion over earth. The Bible says the woman was made for man, not the man made for the woman. Just keeping it into context with the wording of the Bible.

"Wives, submit to your own husbands, as to the Lord. For the husband is head of the wife, as also Christ is head of the church; and He is the Savior of the body. Therefore, just as the church is subject to Christ, so let the wives be to their own husbands in everything. Husbands, love your wives, just as Christ also loved the church and gave Himself for her, that He might sanctify and cleanse her with the washing of water by the word, that He might present her to Himself a glorious church, not having spot or wrinkle or any such thing, but that she should be holy and without blemish. So husbands ought to love their own wives as their own bodies; he who loves his wife loves himself. For no one ever hated his own flesh, but nourishes and cherishes it, just as the Lord does the church. For we are members of His body, of His flesh and of His bones. "For this reason a man shall leave his father and mother and be joined to his wife, and the two shall become one flesh." This is a great mystery, but I speak concerning Christ and the church. Nevertheless let each one of you in particular so love his own wife as himself, and let the wife see that she respects her husband" (Ephesians 5:22-33 NKJV).

The church bears the same title as women, wives and bride. God bears the title husband. So, with the church representing wives and God representing husbands:

Wives = submit to husbands
Church = submit to God

Wives are supposed to submit to husbands as the "scripture states." As the church is supposed to submit to

God, husbands are to love their wives as God loves the church.

God has an order of Authority. Look at any well run organization of government. They have what we call a chain of command. If I have a problem in Atlanta, Georgia at a place of work, I would not go to the corporate office in California if I have a supervisor right at that facility; just like in the armed forces, there is a chain of command. Now, if that chain of command is not following the code of ethics or laws, then that can be a reason to jump that chain of command. A woman can jump that chain also when the man is not following the ways of Christ. However, it still doesn't give her authority over the man, no more than a private has authority over a master Sergeant. If that master Sergeant is doing things detrimental to the safety or well-being of that private, he can report it and fall under the authority of a higher authority if deemed. Just like a woman whose husband is not following the will of God; she falls under the authority of God or even a spiritual leader can be her covering. The Bible clearly speaks about a woman usurping the authority of a man. *"And I do not permit a woman to teach or to have authority over a man, but to be in silence. For Adam was formed first, then Eve. And Adam was not deceived, but the woman being deceived, fell into transgression"* (1 Timothy 2:12-14 NKJV).

Look at any household where a husband and wife are raising a child and the woman is constantly usurping the father's authority. There will be rebellion and chaos in that home and undisciplined children, especially males. If the world is to say a man is to submit to a woman, then that's like saying God is to submit to the church in His established order. The woman came out from the side of man when God put Adam in a deep sleep. The church came out the side of the Son of Man when He was on the cross. They pierced His side and out came blood and water. In order for us to rein in God's church, we need to be baptized with water after repenting our sins. After we experience the water, we are now covered by the blood. We have to be healed of our spiritual blindness (be saved) to even begin to understand the things of revelations of God. Now we become members (a part) of the church, which is the bride, then we submit to the husband, which is God.

I know again the topic of marriage, divorce and remarriage is a hotly debated topic. In the framework in exposing truth, some biblical facts are just as controversial. When it comes to the order of God, it can seem male chauvinist and unfair. Remember God's way is not necessarily man's ways (Isaiah 55:8). A lot of times our thinking is clouded because of sin; unhealthy spiritual relationships and the limited wisdom of man. What we don't understand doesn't mean it is not the perfect will of God.

CHAPTER 5

JOURNEY TO TRUTH

The whole quest in life, as well as your marriage, is to become the best you. Everything is about you. As he will often do, as you delight yourself more and more in him. The more you conform to his ways God speaks. He revealed something very interesting to me. There are people with good hearts, meaning they try to do good, but fall short. Some fall short due to ignorance, but their heart remains soft to be receptive to correction. Even when they do wrong, they have good intentions and they constantly evolve and grow. Sin, all sin has consequences. So that does not mean they escape the consequence, but God is forgiving and just to see them through. These types of people have the ability to self-reflect and lay their lives on the table and be honest. That is what the Sabbath was all about. He created (worked) for six days and on the seventh day He rested to reflect on what He did.

Then there are some people with wicked hearts, meaning they do not try to do what is right. They constantly rebel and refuse to evolve into the righteousness of the light. These are hard hearted people. Their heart is not receptible to correction. They glory in the wickedness and the lies they live. This type of person is in danger of having their minds condemned in damnation (2 Thessalonians 2:12). The Bible says, *"The heart is deceitful above all things, And desperately wicked; Who can know it?"* (Jeremiah 17:9 NKJV).

When I speak of the heart or the Bible, it is talking about the mind. In 2 Peter 1:20-21 (KJV), *"Knowing this first, that no prophecy of the scripture is of any private interpretation. For the prophecy came not in old time by the will of man: but holy men of God spake as they were moved by the Holy Ghost."*

We, as humans, cannot begin to interpret the word of God, decipher right from wrong, or even begin to evolve into holy character beings until we allow a renewing of the mind with God's spirit which is fed daily with His word.

So, the key to life's problems and especially marriage has to start with you. I do not care what someone did to you. I mean this seriously, but in an empathetic way. I sympathize with abuse, adultery, hurt; I honestly do. In all that hurt and all that pain, remember forgiveness is medicine for you, not the offender. Through all that, we must focus on you. It does not matter how many times my wife cheated, the emotional abuse, the lies, manipulation, deception—it does not matter. In focusing on me, I see I did not have an ongoing relationship with God. I esteemed my wife to be higher than God. In doing that, I allowed myself to be incapable to react or respond in a Godly way. I allowed myself to cheat my marriage by not demonstrating Godly love or walking in the counsel of God. I allowed myself to become distracted in the things of God (Nehemiah 6:1-3). I allowed myself to be polluted with bitterness from the first offense to where I became a double minded man not taking care of myself, the temple of God. That goes from not feeding my spirit daily to indulging in alcohol and marijuana. All while the enemy crept in and fortified strongholds.

Even through all this, it does not justify your spouse's wrong doings. I'm simply saying when things go wrong in your relationship, focus on you and weigh out options that you played in the demise. Your spouse has to do the same, but it depends on the condition of the heart. That is what the parable of the sower in Matthew 13 is all about. The seed being the truth, the word of good the different terrains is the condition of one's heart.

I know some are saying how dare you, he abused me. Still concentrate on you. It could be your choice (a spouse totally the opposite of what scripture teaches). Did you have any provocation, not justifying it in any manner?

A person should be able to go out and enjoy yourself without incidence. Common sense tells us that at a certain time you should be careful in the streets. Law enforcement and security can tell us that at a certain time of morning in clubs and in the streets it is a whole other spirit.

The thread I'm trying to weave into every married couple, or soon to be, is: if you follow God's ways of developing character, a holy lifestyle (you), then in turn follow the instructions or blueprint of God's way of dealing with marriage, no marriage should fail.

I. Law of Marriage

To understand the law of marriage, we must first understand a key component in marriage. That key component being love.

Love is a law. *"A new commandment I give unto you, That ye love one another; as I have loved you, that ye also love one another"* (John 13:34 KJV). Love is the most misunderstood word in today's relationships as many today equate it to being a feeling. With that being said, let's highlight some pointers:

- Marriage is an important decision a human will make in life, next to worshipping God.
- Choosing a life partner for marriage must not be taken lightly.
- Marriage is not a requirement.
- God does not choose your mate.
- Love is not the foundation of marriage.
- Love is a key component but is not the foundation of marriage.

Even if a person has graduated from love is a feeling stage. To understand love is a choice, love is a commitment, it still does not mean the marriage will be successful. Love does not hold a marriage together.

The book of scripture tells us to get wisdom. *"Wisdom is the principal thing; therefore get wisdom: and with all thy getting get understanding"* (Proverbs 4:7 KJV).

Wisdom is the understanding of how something is supposed to work. Many marriages fail, not because of love—love could not hold it together anyway. Many people get a divorce but are still in love. So, the love did not hold the marriage together. Something aroused stronger than love.

The problem is stated in Hosea 4:7-8. Men and women lack the knowledge on how to function in marriage. Successful marriages apply the application of knowledge, knowing God's principles (laws) for marriage.

Most marriages fail due to ignorance. However, even in ignorance, we must understand even that is a choice. *"My people are destroyed for the lack of knowledge: because thou hast rejected knowledge, I will also reject thee, that thou shalt be no priest to me: seeing thou hast forgotten the law of thy God, I will also forget thy children"* (Hosea 4:6 KJV).

As equally as many marriages fail due to selfishness. Some people will just reject the truth and do what they **feel** is right.

Again and again we fail to realize marriage is a divine institution of God, governed by divine laws.

One such divine law is love. *"For all the law is fulfilled in one word, even in this; thou shalt love thy neighbour as thyself. But if ye bite and devour one another, take heed that ye be not consumed one of another"* (Galatians 5:14-15 KJV).

There are four types of love:

1) **Philia** - Brotherly love, friendship kind of love.
   - *"Love one another with brotherly affection. Outdo one another in showing honor"* (Romans 12:10 ESV).
   - *"Let brotherly love continue"* (Hebrews 13:1 ESV).
   - *"If anyone says 'I love God,' and hates his brother, he is a liar; for he who does not love his brother whom he has seen cannot love God whom he has not seen"* (1 John 4:20 ESV).
2) **Storage** - Family love, refers to natural or instinctual affection. For example, the love of a parent towards offspring and vice versa.
   - *"We love because he first loved us"* (1 John 4:19 ESV).

- *"Honor your father and your mother, that your days may be long in the land that the Lord your God is giving you"* (Exodus 20:12 ESV).

3) **Eros** - "Passionate love" or romantic love. This type of love was restricted to marriage and was to be experienced by marriage; and can be on a thin line when lost. It can be beautiful, yet powerful if left unchecked outside the confounds of marriage. It can leave one spiritually empty.
    - *"Let marriage be held in honor among all, and let the marriage bed be undefiled, for God will judge the sexually immoral and adulterous"* (Hebrews 13:4 ESV).
    - God's deep love for His people can be seen in the Song of Solomons.

4) **Agape** - Divine love (Selfless). It is defined as the highest form of love which goes beyond emotion. It embraces a universal, unconditional love that transcends and persists regardless of circumstance. For a marriage to thrive, Agape love is essential to overcome any problem in the foreseeable future.

God created marriage as a loyal partnership between a **male** and a **female**.

Marriage is the strong foundation for starting a family.

Sex was to be expressed in marriage to help build intimacy.

Marriage should be parallel or mirror the image of God's covenant relationship with His people. We see this throughout the Bible when the Messiah refers to Himself as the bride, groom, and the kingdom of Heaven as a wedding banquet.

Many people get married for the happiness and love. As we see in the four different types of love, Eros would fall under marriage as well as Agape.

Eros would tie into marriage because we know that it involves sexual intimacy. Falling in line with the instructions or laws of marriage, we know sex before marriage is forbidden.

I understand that in the world we live in it seems impossible or everyone is taking another path. This is solely because we have been programmed to accept the Masse's way of thinking. That is why the Bible says to <u>renew</u> your mind. There was a popular teaching (Pentecostal) going around that whoever you lay with is your husband or wife.

Well, that is a false teaching, but not entirely false. You see, everyone you may have had sex with is not your spouse. However, in the transmittal of fluids, blood and intimacy, you form what are called soul-ties.

Sex is a tridimensional experience: soul, spirit and body. Whenever a person has sex with another person, neurochemical changes occur that encourage emotional bonding (limbic). This is what is known as soul-ties. Every time you do (did) have sex, you have a piece of your partner stay with you (good, bad or ugly). The result of unhealthy soul-ties is that you create a life-long bond through that sexual encounter.

These are the things we have been misinformed about and therefore convinced that sex is strictly a single-dimensional, physical act without any emotional or spiritual connections. The truth of the marriage covenant is interwoven in the scriptures of the Bible just like the garments worn by the Levitical priests. It symbolizes moral integrity and/or holiness. The priests symbolize one who is chosen to represent the most high for the people.

We deal with some touchy topics like abortions as well as marriage, divorce and remarriage. When dealing with hard topics, we (and when I say "we," I mean people who are honestly and truly desiring to know and please Christ) must learn to deal with His Holiness which is a lifestyle and characteristics of God; also, His truth which is His divine word, God is true. We cannot even deal with facts. I know that sounds crazy however beliefs can be about true or false propositions even though a person always accepts them as being a true proposition, being a statement or assertion that expresses a judgment or opinion. Sadly, we, as people, deal with a lot of opinions led by emotions accepted as facts then believing them to be true. As followers of a Holy God, we must deal in the truth which is His word and believe it and act on it. Just like a good game of spades, the spade trumps any other card in the deck. We have to come to the reality that a lot of times in God's kingdom, truth trump's man's clouded vision of truth, traditions and vain beliefs.

II. Why Marriage?

If we believe in a creator who created creation, we must believe in His moral codes for living. A creator who created every living thing with a purpose. Many church organizations, even motivational speakers, have taught on finding your purpose. However, has anyone stopped to ask, "What is the purpose of marriage?" Some psychologists are beginning to question it. We, as human beings, should not take things for granted without question. If a tradition or custom is right, it should withstand the questioning. So, the question is how, then, did the institution of marriage originate? Even if you believe in evolution, think about this. If man appeared by the evolution process, gradually descending through millions of years from some lower than animal species, similar or ancestor to the Anthropoid ape, how and when was the institution of marriage started? And why?

If humans had evolved from lower animal species, brought about without purpose or design by resident forces, devoid of intelligence, if there had been no planned design by an all-intelligent creator, no purpose for which humans were put on Earth, then indeed, we should wonder: Why marriage?

Further proof that man is governed by a moral code of conduct and ethics, which produce character.

The most widely view is that marriage was created for sex and reproduction. However, many people have sex outside of marriage as well as children being born. For the stiff neck, psychological rebellious atheists, and people in general who deny a creator say man evolved from a lower life from a lower life form to a more intelligent species. Even animals reproduce, but they do not marry. Animals react off instincts. Nobody has to teach an animal to walk, eat, hunt, etc. Usually, an animal is up and walking in a few hours or minutes, but not a human. But a human does act on instinct. We have a mind that can create, reason, solve problems, etc.

Now watch what the book of scriptures says in the first chapter. *"And God created great whales, and every living creature that moveth, which the waters brought forth abundantly, after their kind, and every winged fowl after his kind: and God saw that it was good. And God blessed them, saying, Be fruitful, and multiply, and fill the waters in the seas, and let fowl multiply in the earth...cattle, and creeping thing, and the beast of the earth after his kind..."* (Genesis 1:21-25 KJV).

Does this need any further interpretation? God created fish after their particular kind, birds after their particular kind, cattle after their particular kind. Each kind may have varieties, but each reproduces after its own kind. The book of scriptures did not say God created or fish evolved from the animal kind, or birds from the creepy thing of the earth. **They were created after their own kind. Now, what about man?**

"And God said, Let us make man in our image, after our likeness..." (Genesis 1:26-27 KJV). So, God created man in His own image. This refutes the theory that man evolved from some lower form of mammals to the highest of the animals. It says, "God created man, after the God kind."

Whatever God is like, He made man like him—some form of shape.

We need not guess, imagine or create gods in our own image.

It is revealed throughout scripture, God has arms, legs, feet, a mouth, a voice, a nose, two ears, and two eyes. So, man was formed and shaped to look like God.

God is a spirit (John 4:24). He is composed of a spirit, but He is a formed man of dust (matter). When God breathed into man's nostrils, the breath of life, man became a living soul. Man does not have a soul, but is a soul made (shaped) out of dust (matter).

Just these tidbits of revelation has made me say even louder that "church has failed." Just from this learning of God creating everything after its own kind and man does not have an immortal soul.

Consider this: Adam was the first man, which symbolized an earthly man. Christ is considered the second Adam (spiritual) man. This is also seen in the life of man. *"Howbeit that was not first which is spiritual, but that which is natural; and afterward* (by resurrected) *that which is spiritual. The first man is of earth, earthly; the second man* (Christ) *is the Lord from Heaven"* (1 Corinthians 15:46-47 KJV).

God created man after His own kind! Now notice in the creation scripture, God said, "Let **us** make man in **our** image." Since Moses was God inspired to write the first five books, we know his language is Hebrew and the Hebrew word for God is Elohim. Elohim is a nun implying more than one in unity and diversity within the nature of God, Triune creator who covenants to preserve His creation (but not a trinity).

Faith and obedience are like the yin to the yang. They are so intertwined that one is incomplete without the other. The two go together to compose one of the pillars that supports the believer's arsenal of spiritual weapons.

In other words, this is one of the foundations you build your template on (strong, supportive). You must have faith; without it we cannot please God. You must have faith in the holy spirit of God and have faith that the same power dwells in you, which will empower you to do even greater works because God's spirit (lives) dwells in you.

III. Renewing the Mind

If you are married to someone who has the appearance (a form of Godliness), then you are in for a hard time. I just went through the manifestation of a particular sin or sins that plague the marriage covenant, the big one being adultery, which can birth other sins until your marriage is or becomes Satan's playground. You see, adultery can lead to lies, lust, darkness, separation from God, sexual immorality, guilt, suicide, murder, condemned soul, etc. You get the picture.

Then what about those that are in repeated adultery? What about those in the church, but stay or live in adultery? What is their mind thinking?

If you or your spouse are active in a church and you find them or yourself committing the sin of adultery, we must break it down or trouble shoot to find reasonable causes. If you find yourself going to church week after week and you are committing infractions against God's holy covenant, you must first begin with your mind.

There is a difference from making mistakes to knowingly and willfully living in sin. (Romans 12:2)

Do not be conformed to this world but be transformed by the renewal of your mind. We know to be a lover of the world, we become an enemy of Christ. So, to become a friend and not become an enemy, we need to transform our mind (thought process). The mind is much like an engine to a car: the car has a body, but it does not run or manifest motion until it has an engine. The mind is the engine to the body. Whatever the mind is set on, that is what the body is going to do. This is important. Why may you ask? In Romans 12:1-2 (ESV) it says, *"I appeal to you therefore, brothers, by the mercies of God, to present your bodies as a living sacrifice."* The body is alive and every day you walk with Christ, you have to sacrifice the things, the thoughts, the pleasures, and the false doctrine. Now once we sacrifice daily, we can endure sound doctrine and get under right teaching to learn what it means to be holy. Now when we become that living, walking, and talking sacrifice, and learn what it means to be holy, to live holy, we become acceptable to God. Through prayer and lifestyle and when we become and obey this, it is now our spiritual worship.

The spirit precedes the physical. So, if we are not in this state, then everything we do in church is in vain. The spiritual is the seed which produces or manifests a thing in the physical. The word says we have to worship Him in spirit and in truth. If your spirit is not right, chances are you will not be able to accept the truth, if you are even interested.

Secondly, we must look at the environment. Is the church environment conducive to live in sin, or conducive to leave sin? Many churches have this prosperity or no accountability doctrine. If I am on a hiking trip and lose my map, I can no longer read my map. Chances are I am going to get lost. Many church goers are lost because the preacher, bishop, and/or pastor are unable to decipher and break down God's map thus the congregation is lost unless someone (God led, God anointed) comes along and points you in the right direction.

The Bible clearly tells us to point out sin and separate from it.

"preach the word; be ready in season and out of season; reprove, rebuke, exhort, with great patience and instruction" (2 Timothy 4:2 NASB). *"All Scripture is inspired by God and profitable for teaching, for reproof, for correction..."* (2 Timothy 3:16). If we know that brother or sister is at fault (sin), how many of us have the boldness of God's holy spirit to approach such one? How many of us are not even living anything on our own to not feel guilt? This is a main problem I see in today's churches—instead of against sin, they accept sin. Sadly, many believe they can live anyway they want because Jesus paid the price and redeemed us from sin. No man can live holy! No matter what we do because we are covered by the blood.

In Jude verse three, here he is talking about salvation, something the true saints had in common. Jude is telling them to contend earnestly for the faith. He then goes on to warn them about people who turned the grace of God into licentiousness (lacking willpower; unwilling to conform to God's law usually dealing with promiscuous sex). He goes on to say in verse five that I remind you that the Lord, after saving his people out of the land of Egypt (sin) subsequently (after the saving happened) destroyed those that did not believe.

There is another scripture in Matthew 7:21-23 (NJKV), *"Not everyone who says to Me, 'Lord, Lord' will enter the kingdom of heaven, but the ones who does the will of My father who is in heaven will enter...depart from Me, you who practice lawlessness!"* This scripture right here set off red flags and gave me the decisive to find out what is it that the true and living God requires for me to be saved. Evidently, these people thought they were saved and doing work in the Father's name, so why did He say depart from Me you workers of lawlessness?

"For if, after they have escaped the pollutions of the world through the knowledge of the Lord and Savior Jesus Christ, they are again entangled in them and overcome, the latter end is worse for them than the beginning. For it would have been better for them not to have known the way of righteousness, than having known it, to turn from the holy commandment delivered to them. But it has happened to them according to the true proverb: 'A dog returns to his own vomit,' and, 'a sow, having washed, to her wallowing in the mire'" (2 Peter 2:20-22 NKJV).

"But when a righteous man turns away from his righteousness and commits iniquity, and does according to all the abominations that the wicked man does, shall he

live? All the righteousness which he has done shall not be remembered; because of the unfaithfulness of which he is guilty and the sin which he has committed, because of them he shall die. Yet you say, 'The way of the Lord is not fair.' Hear now, O house of Israel, is it not My way which is fair, and your ways which are not fair? When a righteous man turns away from his righteousness, commits iniquity, and dies in it, it is because of the iniquity which he has done that he dies" (Ezekiel 18:24-26 NKJV).

We see from scripture that 'once saved, always saved' cannot be true, but many live like it is and that is because they are deceived.

It does not even make sense as much as you are a parent to your child when that child is outside of your good graces and abuse your grace. They just keep being disobedient. Are you going to say, "It's okay, you can do what you want?" No, it is time for reproof, rebuke, and correction!

You might be saying, "Whew, but what does this have to do with marriage?" If you were asking that question, then I rest my case. We do not understand the marriage covenant. If the marriage covenant is a divine institution established by a divine God, who is holy, then would it not behoove us to be holy (set apart, consecrated) to enjoy the benefits of a holy matrimony? We will be infused with God's holy spirit and wisdom to deal with any problem or attack that comes up against over marriage.

See, men know how to submit, but not love. Women know how to love, but not submit. See, God knew this, that is why He said it in Ephesians 5:22-25 (NKJV), *"Wives, submit to your own husbands...Husbands love your wives, just as Christ also loved the church..."* Jesus was the ultimate submitter as He submitted His will to the will of the Father. God is love, so He is the author of it.

Rather you believe in different names, religions, or beliefs, can we agree on the moral code embedded throughout religion?

False religion crept in. *"So the great dragon was cast out, that serpent of old, called the Devil and Satan, who deceives the whole world; he was cast to the earth, and his angels were cast out with him"* (Revelations 12:9 NKJV).

The false church started in 33 A.D. by Simon the Sorcerer, described in the 8th chapter of the Book of Acts. As the leader of the Babylonian mystery religion in Samaria, they were gentiles who inhabited the land to the northern Palestine, however the Jews of Sudan would have nothing to do with them. This is recorded in 2 Kings 17:23-24 which is where they settled.

CHAPTER 6

PRAYER

When you are depressed, you need another perspective. Prayer is how we contact or tap into what God has already declared.

Prayer is the absolute necessary tool (weapon), mechanism, etc. that we, as believers, use to release what God has already declared.

Prayer does not make God do what He has not already intended to do. Prayer lets God release what He already intended to do. Cause and effect.

Everything in your life, in this world, has already been decreed from the beginning. To receive the things of God you have to be tapped into the wisdom or knowledge of God. The root word of knowledge is "know." In Genesis 4:1-2 (KJV), *"And Adam **knew** Eve his wife; and she conceived, and bare Cain, and said, I have gotten a man from the Lord..."* The word knew or know is equated to having sex (intimacy with someone).

One of the keys to powerful, purposeful prayer is the intimacy one experiences with the creator. There are many references to what this looks like throughout the Bible (Book of Scriptures). *"...The effectual fervent prayer of the righteous man availeth much"* (James 5:16 KJV).

Effectual prayer is not what "availeth much," but prayer that "availeth much" is "effectual."

The content of James 5:16 is praying for one another, especially those struggling physically and spiritually. In James 5:17, it says Elijah was a man with a nature like ours (he had struggles in the flesh). We see he fervently prayed that it might not rain. The result: it did not rain for three years and six months. So, in taking the meaning of these words as close to the original, we see:

Effectual - Producing an effect; power to produce an effect.
Fervent - Boiling, hot, glowing, figuratively violent, furious, impassioned.

- Prayer many not always be effectual.
- To be effectual, prayer should be passionate.
- You cannot have prayers that have value or worth without it being something you are passionately concerned about.

The effectual, fervent prayer of the righteous man availeth much.

Note: Sometimes to get a better understanding of a quote, I break down the meaning of words. This allows me to break down the sentence close to the meaning of the original sentence.

The power to produce passionate prayer is an outcome of being morally justified and the prayers profit or benefit much.

To be morally justified, one must line up with the D.N.A, the characteristics of a living God. His code of morality, values, and ethics that are written in the laws of the universe. Cause and effects. (Things we do have certain outcomes.) The universal laws operate on the principles of universal order and truth.

I. The Wills of God

Just like any other topic in the Bible, when it comes to the will of God, there are many different opinions and interpretations. While some believe there is just one will of God, some believe there are many wills of God. Let's agree to live a victorious life. It is critical that we learn what the will of God is for our life. Most people do not even know where to begin or struggle to understand God's will.

We tend to start looking at our own lives and questioning: how can it be the will of God to lose a marriage, lose a job, or a loved one? How is it that when we attend churches someone knows the will of God for my life, but I do not? Beware of anyone dressing up their opinion as the will of God.

Much of the confusion about God's will goes back to not understanding God Himself. People discrediting a universal code of human conduct men should live by, as a mere control tactic.

Note: When talking about the permissive will of God, I do not take the view some theologies view as God being impotent to do anything about human sin. This view makes man sovereign, not God.

The permissive—will of God—some theologians argue if this is even biblical. As some argue their point based on the note above, it makes man sovereign over God. The word permissive (permission) means to permit or suggest some sort of positive action. People can easily get confused and believe God has no power over sin (He permits what He cannot help, but permits because He has no sovereign power over it).

God's permissible will is the way things play out. Nothing is outside of God's permissible will. He permits suffering at times, but He always has a plan. (Everything is working for His glory, will, and plan.) So to say the whole permissible will is not biblical is a stretch. What about every time you fall short, but keep getting up or chastised to repentance? God does not cause the suffering, but He will allow it. Remember the story of Job.

"And we know that for those who love God all things work together for good, for those who are called according to his purpose" (Romans 8:28 ESV).

The key to understanding is humbleness. The key to wisdom is fear God.

The fact is many of us do not have enough word in us to know the will of God let alone understand it. When we hear things that challenge the way we believe, or have been taught, we become close minded and no longer interested in the truth, but satisfied with living life based on your truths. And once again most of us do not even know the will of good, the ways of good to even discern the things of God. In the Book of Acts, the Apostle Paul had a scenario where he had to deal with two types of spirits, two types of mindsets. When I speak in these terms of spirits and mindsets, I am not adding or taking away. Just simply expounding of the scripture with a deeper meaning.

In Acts 17:11 (KJV), we see the mindset of the Bereans, *"These were more noble than those in Thessalonica, in fact they received the word with all readiness of mind, and searched the scriptures daily, whether those things were so."* Versus the mindset of the Thessalonica we see in verse two and five of the same chapter. *"And Paul, as his manner was, went in unto them, and three sabbath days reasoned with them out of the scriptures,"* (Acts 17:2 KJV). Unlike the Bereans, who accepted his teaching had enough study themselves to know scripture. As a result, they compared teaching to scripture, whereas with the Thessalonica's, Paul had Sabbath days. Some envied the truth and was struck in their ways and traditions. Which spirit are you?

"But the Jews which believed not, moved with envy, took unto them certain lewd fellows of the baser sort, and gathered a company, and set all the city on an uproar,..." (Acts 17:5 KJV).

Some people will do awful, and selfish things to cling to a belief than realize change is necessary and the best thing.

Spiritual blindness was not always physical, but mental, which leads to spiritual deaf. Notice how Satan (demonic leads) is characterized as a snake. When a snake attacks its prey, it squeezes the life out (breaths) and attacks the head. It devours from the head down. Just like demonic spirits; they attack from the head (mind). Control the mind (you). Control the body (deeds).

CHAPTER 7

THE PAULINE PRIVILEGE

The Pauline Privilege is the allowance by the Roman Catholic Church of the dissolution of marriage of two persons not baptized at the time the marriage occurred. The Pauline Privilege is drawn from the apostle Paul instructions in the first Epistle to the Corinthians.

This is the definition of Pauline Privilege and it is basically self-explanatory to the reader. This is the interpretation and/or teaching that has had some traction in the churches either directly or indirectly.

This doctrine has become known as the marriage clause (an expectation) to the rule if two people have gotten married before being baptized (saved, live for God). You can imagine the friction between a saved and unsaved person, so the clause permits for divorce. But is this truly biblical and in harmony with all the other rules in marriage?

1 Corinthians 7:11-15 (RSV) seems to support this belief. *"...But if the unbelieving partner desires to separate, let it be so; in such a case the brother or sister is not bound. For God has called us to peace."*

When we deal with truth and God's word, remember Jesus (Messiah) did not come to bring peace, but a sword. Truth will divide families! This verse (1 Corinthians 7:11-15) is being interpreted that if you're in a marriage and your unbelieving spouse wants to leave you, you can let them leave and you are not under bondage to this marriage. Thus, they can or are free to divorce and remarry.

Okay, let's see what the author of marriage says with the scripture Matthew 19:3-6 (KJV), *"The Pharisees also came unto him, tempting him, and saying unto him, Is it lawful for a man to put away his wife for every cause? And he answered and said unto them, Have ye not read, that he when made them at the beginning made them male and female. And said, For this cause shall a man leave father and mother, and shall cleave to his wife: and they twain shall be one flesh? Wherefore they are more twain, but one flesh. What therefore God hath joined together, let not man put asunder."*

In this scripture we see who instituted marriage. We see the participants and how it was in the beginning. Marriage was always considered a bond, as the meaning of bond is as follows:

Bond - A thing used to tie something or fasten things together/promise/pledge/vow.

We see in verse four where we are to leave our original family to form our own, by becoming one with your spouse. If we were following the instructions of the scripture, we should be starving to be God-like and living more holy so that when we unite with someone with scripture credentials, we can reproduce after its own kind. This can be an explanation for what we call generational curses, but when we become enlightened, all curses can be broken. In verse six, we see God make a declaration that marriage is a divine institution where you make vows to a holy God. He states that whatever He has joined together let no man put asunder (to divide, separate). In verse ten, it furthers expounds on the seriousness and limited options when it came to being married in honoring your vow. *"His disciples say unto him,*

If the case of the man be so with his wife, it is not good to marry" (Matthew 19:10 KJV).

They said it in amazement or as a sense of seriousness. If the Messiah taught first and foremost what the Pharisees wanted the word to interpret, that you can marry then divorce for any reason, don't you think the disciples' statement in verse ten would be relevant? If divorce and remarriage was what He taught, then it seems to me, marriage would not be all that bad. I mean, you fail at one (or tired of), you are free to dump and move on. By the way, the majority of the world is living like that now. However, could their statement be because of how stringent marriage was truly taught? The Pharisees wanted many ways to divorce; the Messiah taught one. *"And I say unto you, Whosoever shall put away his wife, except it be for fornication, and shall marry another, committeth adultery: and whoso marrieth her which is put away doth commit adultery"* (Matthew 19:9 KJV). We will label this scripture Exhibit A for future reference.

I open my case on this Matthew chapter 19 and some key scripture because it shows:

1. Man has been trying to distort this teaching
2. Who established marriage
3. The original participates
4. Man's government has no authority over

- We see in verse three the Pharisees came to tempt or test the Messiah.
- In verse four, we see how God established marriage from the beginning also the original participates.
- In verse six, we see where God says, "What therefore God hath joined together, let no man put

asunder!" This is a starting line on the covenant of marriage.

Now back to 1 Corinthians 7:15 which is where I believe is the only scripture the Pauline Privilege was founded. It says, *"But if the unbeliever departs, let him depart; a brother or a sister is not under bondage in such cases. But God has called us to peace"* (NKJV).

We will call this the evidence presented. My opening argument is simply this:

Some have argued that 1 Corinthians 7:15 provides a second cause for divorce (in addition to the "fornication" of Matthew 19:9, Exhibit A) and so, by implication, expands Jesus' teaching and authorizes a subsequent remarriage on the grounds of desertion by an unbelieving mate. This is commonly known as the Pauline Privilege that we see to correctly divide the word of God.

This theory is certainly not new. It was advocated by Chrysostom (C.A.D. 347-407), one of the so called "church fathers." It became part of Roman Catholic canon law and was defended by Martin Luther. I seek to demonstrate that this view is unwarranted and constitutes a compromise of the creator's teaching on divorce and remarriage. This theory reads into the context that simply is not there.

Here are the facts:

Was Paul teaching different than what Christ taught? The answer is no; regarding divorce, Christ had spoken comprehensively (Matthew 5:31-32, 19:9). The subject being reviewed in 1 Corinthians 7:10-15 was not about divorce. The Corinthian Saints were asking many questions relating to marriage; Corinth was wicked morally and worldly.

However, you had many people converting to the faith. In return, you see a lot of marriages and families consisting of believers and non-believers. This fact alone caused strive and this is what they were dealing with.

Here are some of the questions they were asking:

Should a Christian husband and wife separate from (Chorizo) or leave (Aphiemi) each other (1 Corinthians 7:10-11)? Paul's answer was no. But should a separation occur, celibacy should be maintained or else a reconciliation affected.

Should a Christian leave his unbelieving mate? Again, Paul's response was no, not if the unbeliever is willing to remain with the believer (1 Corinthians 7:12-13).

What if the unbeliever initiates a separation? What should the Christian do? Let him go, the apostle says. The Christian is not enslaved (bondage) to that mate in the sense that domestic proximity is absolutely required (1 Corinthians 7:15). "Divorce" is not under consideration here. The New Testament term for divorce is "apoluo" (literally to lose away, Matthew 5:31-32, 19:3,7-9) and that word is avoided in 1 Corinthians 7:10-15.

Paul makes it clear that the general theme under consideration in this context had not been comprehensively dealt with by the Lord. The Lord had taught concerning some matters *"not I, but the Lord"* (1 Corinthians 7:10), but not with reference to their matters *"say I, not the Lord"* (1 Corinthians 7:12).

The word rendered "bondage" (1 Corinthians 7:15) is the Greek term "douloo," which means "to make a slave." Observe how the word is used in Titus 2:3 - "enslaved to much wine."

Speaking on a view of marriage from the scriptures it never speaks to it as being slavery. The "bondage" (enslavement), does not refer to the marriage union. If the unbeliever departs, that is not the Christian's responsibility. The brother or sister is not enslaved or under bondage to maintain a unity (1 Corinthians 7:15) at the expense of your relationship with God.

The word "douloo" (under bondage) in verse 15 is, in the Greek testament, a perfect tense form, "dedoulutai." The perfect tense denotes a present state resulting from past action. Its force here is this was not bound (past action) and is not bound (present tense). A better sense of the verse is:

Yet if (assuming such should occur), the unbeliever separates himself, let him separate himself; the brother or sister was not (before departure) and is not (now that the departure occurred) enslaved. Whatever the **bondage** is, therefore, the Christian was not in it even before the disgruntled spouse left. But the Saint was married (and is) to him, hence the bondage, not the marriage.

1 Corinthians 7:15 does not expand upon the Savior's teachings with the reference to divorce and remarriage, as much as some wish that it were. The Pauline Privilege is derived in the imagination of men's minds. It goes to show what is happening in the spirit realm. If marriage once again is the "physical" example of our relationship with our God, then the relationship between God and mankind is in a divorced state. It shows how lack of knowledge and understanding has led to the downfall of man as far as morals, integrity, and values. The power of the church is diminished because they accept, teach, and preach these lies. We are in a war, yet it being spiritual, which makes it greater. Prayer is the most powerful weapon of God and His word is like ammunition.

If the word we are putting out is false, then it is like shooting blanks. You are in a war, your enemy is shooting real bullets and you are shooting blanks. It is non-effective, just like the word from the pulpits. Sure, they are packed with people. Is it for entertainment, singing, emotions, or to truly learn truth and really apply it to our lives? Do we get just as enthused for the truth of God? Now that some light was shown on 1 Corinthians 7:15, let's look at Matthew 19:9, which is considered the first clause for divorce and in many beliefs the only clause. Just like the understanding in the 1 Corinthians 7:15 is often misinterpreted, let's see if this is so in the case of Matthew 19:9.

We know Corinths was a wicked village where many were converting over to the faith the Apostles taught. This was causing friction in the marriages between one being saved and the other unsaved.

We know bondage (slavery) was never synonymous with marriage.

We know from Matthew 19:8, Moses permitted divorce. Why? Because of the condition of the people's heart (hard-hearted) when a person is not living according to God's will, it is the heart that is described as darkened, rebellious, callous, unfeeling, or idolatrous. It is within the heart that God works; hence the human heart may be tender and soft or as hard as stone (Ezekiel 11:19). It is in this context that hardening or hardness of the heart must be understood. The heart represents the tote. One response of a person of a person to life around him or her and to the religious and moral demands of God. Hardness of heart thus describes a negative condition in which the person ignores, spurns, or rejects the gracious off of God to be part of his or her life. In Matthew 19:8, the Messiah states this condition and also states that from the beginning it was not so. He not only states that in the beginning it was not like this, but in verse nine He comes along and re-establishes this order from the beginning by saying, *"I tell you that anyone who divorces his wife except for fornication, and marries another commits adultery."*

Here goes the original (except, but) clause that the whole word who engages in divorce agrees that this clause is valid. Along with abandonment (which we just explored) and abuse, many believe that once married one can divorce if they're spouse steps out. Many agree that only the offended party is free to divorce. So believe both are free and the marriage dissolved.

I would now like to take this time and identify two classes of people with two words that are similar, but yet different due to the status of a person.

The first one being:

Fornicator - which leads to the act of fornication. A fornicator is a person who is not married or never been married who engages in the act of sex. Simple terms, sex outside of marriage.

Adulterer - which leads to the act of adultery. And an adulterer is a person who is married and engaged in a sexual act with someone outside of their marriage.

Two words similar in that they both are sexual sins unto the body, yet different considering the status of the person committing it.

When we understand, remember the book of scripture commands that in all our getting an understanding (Proverbs 4:7), and read Matthew 19:9 we understand that it offers a contradiction at first glance. *"And I say to you: whoever divorces his wife except for sexual immorality and marries another, commits adultery."*

The original translation for "sexual immorality" is fornication. It was later translated sexual immorality to include different types of sexual acts, bestiality, homosexuality, etc.

From our definitions, we see that married people "do not" commit fornication. The Greek word for this is "porneia." So, we see some contradiction to just accept it means you can simply dissolve your marriage because of infidelity.

Upon further study if we examine the relationship of Joseph and Mary. A real example of someone who experienced the meaning of this scripture. In Luke 1:26-27 (KJV) we see, *"And in the sixth month the angel Gabriel was sent from God unto a City of Galilee, named Nazareth. To a virgin espoused to a man whose name was Joseph."* The angel continues in verse 30 and 31, *"And the angel said unto her, Fear not Mary: for thou hast found favour with God. And, behold, thou shalt conceive in thy womb, and bring forth a son, and shalt call his name Jesus."*

In verse 27, we see the relationship between Mary and Joseph. She was an espoused wife to Joseph. The word espoused is an ancient custom of Israel. The groom paid a bridal price, and they were considered husband and wife except they did not have sexual relations until the groom finished preparations and came to take her home. It means to cause a girl to be engaged to a man. It is also considered a time for preparing oneself.

So now if we put Matthew 19:9 in content with the Israel custom of espousal and the act of fornication relating to sexual transgression in a marriage, the espousal period was the period of engagement. Two people are still single but make a commitment to marriage. So, when we make the scriptures harmonize, we see that during the espousal period, it was a period of preparation and proving worthiness before the actual marriage. The man honored this commitment by paying a bridal price. This scripture says if a man finds his wife unclean (sexual impunity) he can put her away and vice versa. The law of God is for all men (humanity). It is during this period of commitment, engagement that if one is found guilty of fornication, sexual immorality (which broadens it to other types of sexual acts, bestiality, pornography, etc.), the spouse is legally allowed to "put the other away." It does not mean once one is **married**!

What God has joined together, let no man put asunder. (2 Samuel 3:14, Matthew 1:18, Luke 1:27-2:5, Song of Solomon 3:11, Jeremiah 2:2, 2 Corinthians 11:2)

Greek for "apoluo" from 575 and 3089; = to free, to let go, loose, and divorce.

I. Understanding Sin and the Law

- Sin is transgression of the law.
- The law is God's order and principles on how things are to operate from nature to man.

There are three kinds of laws that the book of scriptures deals with:

1. Civil laws - these were specifically given for the culture of the Israelites, known as laws of the land.
2. Ceremonial laws - these were the customs of a nation, these included old testament sacrifices.
3. God's (moral) law - these relate to justice and judgement. They are based on God's own holy nature. Moral law encompasses regulations on justice, respect and sexual conduct. Humanity will be accountable to these laws.

Out of these three laws it is God's moral law which is unchanging and based on the highest nature of man which is spiritual. In 1 Corinthians 6:9-11, it deals with God's moral law. It tells how the unrighteous should not inherit the kingdom of God. This includes fornicators, idolaters, adulterers, effeminates, homosexuals, thieves, coveters, drunkards, or extortioners. In verse 11, it tells us we can be justified and sanctified through His word and that's good news.

Out of sins we see through scripture there are seven God hate, which are listed below with variant acts that can fall under each.

- **Pride** - unrepenting heart, vanity, stubbornness
- **Envy** - hate, jealousy, coveting
- **Gluttony** - drunkenness, over indulge
- **Greed** - love for money, idolatry
- **Lust** - adultery, fornication, (spiritual and physical)
- **Slothfulness** - lazy, idleness
- **Wrath** - anger, murder, abuse

Even though this developed from Christian theology, the Bible speaks of abominations in Proverbs 6:16-19. Also, we can see the sins which spawn off of each one of these conditions (mindset).

Adultery is one of the worst things that can happen to a marriage. It violates everything you've known and built with your spouse on a very intimate personal level. Cheating is one of the easiest ways to damage a relationship. It completely shatters the basic foundation of a relationship which is trust.

There are two types of adultery:

Physical - which is when a married person has sexual relations outside of their marriage.

Spiritual - which is when a person indulges in false Doctrine, false entities and lives a life totally contrary to the way of God.

Not only is adultery severe and devastating, it is also running rapper and leading to a violent act (tearing apart, separating) which is divorce. If that which is planted in the spiritual is birthed in the physical and adultery is manifested at an alarming rate in the physical, it should send warning signs to the state of the world's spiritual condition. Some of the most obvious consequences of adultery may include:

- Illness - there is growing evidence of a discovered affair can lead to post traumatic stress, exposed to sexually transmitted diseases
- Divorce - most people divorce as the death of betrayal and emotional pain seems unbearable
- Loss of trust and intimacy - adultery causes loss of trust and loss of intimacy
- Guilt/Shame - is big in adultery; most times we think it's just the cheater but the victim can feel bouts of shame

The fatal blow to any marriage is an adulterous affair where one or both spouses think they finally found his or her soulmate. Once this false conception of marriage, 'that you married the wrong spouse or that God put someone new in your life' - with that mindset the ideal of divorce can take root and blossom. In today's world, adultery is typically viewed as nothing more than sexual intercourse outside of marriage. If adultery however is perceived solely as a physical act, its devastation should be relatively simple to deal with as it would basically consist of the offending party to ask for forgiveness and recommit to the marriage. The deception is such a recovery even though many marriages may operate like this, is that it fails to realize that adultery involves much more than a sexual act. It is also a betrayal of a sacred covenant and a violation of one's oath to be faithful. Additionally, adultery is always, "say always" associated with other sins. If this sinful linkage is overlooked, any remedy for marriage restoration will often prove to be superficial since it disregards the need for repentance of all related sins. It will also fail to address the consequences of adultery that impact other people and areas of life. Adultery is compared to idolatry as seen in Jeremiah chapter 3, also in Ezekiel 23:37 (ESV), *"for they have committed adultery, and blood is on their hands. With their idols they have committed adultery..."* Adultery and idolatry are similar because they are both self-centered acts of faithless treachery.

When I said many sins accompany adultery keep in mind first, people who neglect or depart from God's will (ways) can be susceptible to commit any number of sins without remorse. In Proverbs 6:16-19 (ESV), the Messiah shows us sins of abomination that the Lord hates. *"There are six things that the Lord hates, seven that are an abomination to him: haughty eyes, a lying tongue, and hands that shed innocent blood, a heart that devises wicked plans, feet that make haste to run to evil, a false witness who breathes out lies, and one who sows discord among brothers."*

Can you see some of the abominations that spawn from adultery?

Haughty eyes (Job 24:15) - the eye of the adulterer waits for the Twilight saying no eye will see me and he disguises his face.

Lying tongue (Proverbs 12:19) - the lip of truth shall be established forever; but a lying tongue is but for a moment.

A heart that devises wicked plans (Proverbs 6:18) - a heart that devises wicked plans, feet that are swift in running to evil.

Feet that make haste to run to evil (Proverbs 7:11, see Proverbs 6:18) - she is loud and rebellious her feet would not stay home.

Adultery is an entanglement of lust (I desire) coveting (I deserve) and pride (I demand). Anyone who commits adultery lacks understanding, that person cannot avoid inevitable personal consequences nor anticipate the agonizing heartache that others impacted by adultery will experience.

The curse of humanity is death. The scriptures equate sin and death as inseparable; the two go hand-in-hand. When we look at the word death, a biblical explanation of the word is separation. When the body dies, the soul separates from the body which therefore experiences death. When we separate from God's daily word and His ways, we suffer a spiritual death or separation from God. Any illegitimate separation equals death. Death doesn't mean something has ended but something has separated. Most marriages suffer because they experience a spiritual death. This disconnect or separation is a separation from God in the form of disobedience.

II. The Law of Separation

"And did not he make one? (union with wife) *Yet had he the residue of the spirit. And wherefore one? That he might seek a godly seed. Therefore take heed to your spirit, and let none deal treacherously against the wife of his youth"* (Malachi 2:15 KJV).

In prior versus, specifically Malachi 2:10-16, God accuses Israel of being unfaithful to each other. The highlight of these versus was men were divorcing their wives. In verse 14, we see that this is offensive to God. *"Yet ye say, Wherefore? Because the Lord hath been witness between thee and the wife of thy youth, against whom thou hast dealt treacherously: yet is she thy companion, and the wife of thy covenant"* (Malachi 2:14 KJV).

It was considered offensive to God because such vows are made in His presence. Divorce as seen in verse 15 is described as a spiritual failure. This is repeated and magnified in verse 16. Also in the way the men of Israel were divorcing their wives in order to marry pagans was considered foul to God; pagan meaning they worship other Gods and beliefs. (Malachi 2:11) Rather than acting like heads and protectors, these divorcing men were committing acts of spiritual violence against their wives. This condition to me is a manifestation of their spiritual connection to God, which they knew of the Messiah but had no relationship. In verse 15, there is a clear sense in this verse that God is involved in the concept of marriage. This verse is in the context of men being faithless to their wives through divorce. In contrast, God sees marriage as a joining of spirits according to His will, which can't be broken without spiritual damage. God has specific purposes for marriage which are thwarted by divorce. These scriptures are the strongest Bible indicator of God's view on divorce and in no uncertain terms, Malachi expresses God's hatred for divorce.

"And unto the married I command, yet not I, but the Lord, Let not the wife depart from her husband:" (1 Corinthians 7:10 KJV).

We see in this verse of scripture what the Lord desires: 'wife do not depart from your husband.'

As we continue to verse 11, we see it begins with a big ole **but. BUT - used to introduce a clause contrasting with what has already been mentioned.**

Verse 11 is an introduction to a clause with a contrasting view to verse 10. *"But and if she departs, let her remain unmarried or be reconciled to her husband: and let not the husband put away his wife"* (1 Corinthians 7:11 KJV).

In verse 11, we see the clause to verse 10 which is the law of separation. If she departs (separate), let her remain unmarried. In the case her spouse is still living and she decides to have a companion, the word of God says to reconcile with your husband. These scriptures are really self-explanatory so what is it we the world are missing? So many people, male and female, rush to be in another or other relationships that they further damage any reconciliation, but most importantly the spiritual damage we inflict on ourselves. I gave some interesting facts on how we have basically all the elements in our body which are in the earth. The scripture say we were made from dust and clay on a potter's wheel. So, in retrospect, if we are made from the very element we sin against, then do we become the instigator of the whole cause and effect (we sin against the very earth we are made from) from a spiritual viewpoint? Like I previously stated, marriage is a God divine institution governed by God's divine law. Where a man and woman comply to honor their vows, learn and live a Godly life, and raise Godly offspring, recreating God's image in the earth to prepare us for judgment and being accepted in God's Divine family.

With all that being said, one can still make an argument for this next scripture. *"I gave faithless Israel her certificate of divorce and sent her away because of all her adulteries. Yet I saw that her unfaithful sister Judah had no fear; she also went out and committed adultery"* (Jeremiah 3:8 NIV).

My defensive argument could suddenly sink the same God in Malachi 2:16 says God hates divorce to the same God in Jeremiah 3:8 that divorced his bride. Just like anything else or any other scripture, it has to flow in content. You have to be inspired by a divine God to put the puzzle together like legos. Every time a man or woman of God says something recorded in scripture makes it true, but it does not make it righteous.

Job said to the lord giveth, the lord taketh away (Job 1:20-21). He thought his misfortune was because of God. Some turned this into a doctrine. Now we believe our misfortune comes from God. So, we become desensitized to the fact our misfortunes come because of our decisions and actions. This in turns speaks to our obedience or disobedience. It should be noted some attacks are spiritual.

Trials produce character.

Samson was disobedient to God's ways. He was sleeping with a woman he was not married to. (How else are you going to tell your secret?) David fooled around with a married woman, the result was a dead husband, dead baby, and a severe relationship with God. Solomon had many wives, Abraham lied, etc.

We see consistent behavior that was short of God's standard and was not considered right by Creert men. Even in their shortcomings, we see a harmonious beat of love, forgiveness and reconciliation. Back to Jeremiah 3.

Verse 1 (NKJV): *"They say, 'If a man divorces his wife, And she goes from him And becomes another man's* (wife)*, May he return to her again? Would not that land be greatly polluted? But you have played the harlot with many lovers; Yet return to Me,' says the Lord."*

Here God was stating the Mosaic Law and the answer was no. A man who had divorced his wife could not later remarry her.

"When a man takes a wife and marries her, and it happens that she finds no favor in his eyes because he has found some uncleanness in her, and he writes her a certificate of divorce, puts it in her hand, and sends her out of his house, when she has departed from his house, and goes and becomes another man's wife, if the latter husband detests her and writes her a certificate of divorce, puts it in her hand, and sends her out of his house, or if the latter husband dies who took her as his wife, then her former husband who divorced her must not take her back to be his wife after she has been defiled..." (Deuteronomy 24:1-4 NKJV).

It should be noted here that there is a difference between the ideal that God made "from the beginning" and what He allowed and regulated after sin entered the picture. From the beginning, God's desire for marriage was for there to be one man and woman joined by Him. Sin came into the picture and corrupted the arrangement.

(Hardness of Hearts) God's answer to bring things back to the beginning was Christ. What God desires is what is found "from the beginning" and made anew in Christ. What

God permitted and regulated are for the hardness of hearts. While now commanding all to repent (Acts 17:30-31). Although, this is not a fair representation of what God desires and sets straight through **Jesus Christ**.

We see in Jeremiah 3:6-10 (NKJV), God speaks to Jeremiah about backsliding Israel and a treacherous Judah. *"The Lord said also to me in the days of Josiah the king: 'Have you seen what backsliding Israel has done? She has gone up on every high mountain and under every green tree, and there played the harlot. And I said, after she had done all these things, 'Return to Me.' But she did not return. And her treacherous sister Judah saw it. Then I saw that for all the causes for which backsliding Israel had committed adultery, I had put her away and given her a certificate of divorce; yet her treacherous sister Judah did not fear, but went and played the harlot also. So it came to pass, through her casual harlotry, that she defiled the land and committed adultery with stones and trees* (false idols). *And yet for all this her treacherous sister Judah has not turned to Me with her whole heart, but in pretense,' says the Lord.'"*

1) *"In the days of Josiah the king"* - Josiah was king of Judah. During his reign, there was an all out crusade to rid Israel of idolatry.
2) *"Have you seen what backsliding Israel has done?"* - The prophecy of the northern kingdom of Israel was idolatrous. Yet, we see God still called to them saying, "return to me."
3) *"Her treacherous sister Judah saw it"* - Judah of the southern kingdom did not heed to the lessons learned from Israel's refusal to repent. Yet, her

treacherous sister Judah did not fear, but went and played the harlot also.

Can I take a minute to pause? I just see a lot going on just in this passage of scripture (Jeremiah 3:6-10). These incidents, character and behavior can be seen in today's society. We have a disobedient covenant breaking Israel in all her haughtiness. Play the harlot by seeking relationships outside of their marriages. When these relationships include sex, we are now an adulterer, just like Israel. Just like Judah, man can see the destruction and arrogance of his own way and still choose to live in the flesh (calamity) and feel good over doing right. I can see the offense of idolatry, putting anything before **you and your God.** This is personal to me as I can say I am guilty of that.

> 4) <u>"Yet for all this her treacherous sister Judah has not turned to Me with her whole heart, but in pretense."</u>
> - It seemed that Judah had not learned anything from the sin and consequences that came upon Israel. Their repentance was not from the whole heart, but only in pretense.

Through all this God granted a certificate of divorce through Mosaic Law and according to Mosaic Law (Deuteronomy 24:1-9), if a man divorced his unfaithful wife, he is not to take her back. So, Israel seemed hopeless. She has been divorced by God, and according to the law, she can never be accepted back. Okay, I want you to examine this and meditate on this, let it soak in. Study the behavior of Israel, then Judah.

But then comes a surprising phenomenon. God's mercy intervenes in Jeremiah 3:12 (ESV), **"Return, faithless Israel, declares the Lord...I will not be angry forever."**

God commands them three times to come back after He says He divorces them.

God's goodness is found in Hosea which God commanded to marry a prostitute (Hosea 1-2). God's purpose was to show the greatness of His grace. *"...Love her as the Lord loves the Israelites, though they turned to other gods..."* (Hosea 3:1 NIV).

How can a divorced wife return and be restored? Law forbade it, but "mercy triumphs over judgement" (James 2:13). And God still has a plan for Israel, God's grace in the new covenant provided restoration for all who would believe Christ. Marriage is restored to the beginning through Christ. God describes His relationship to Israel as being married to a backslider. Divorce is a form of backsliding. All other scripture pertaining to putting away is a form of separation. Divorce and separation are not the same. Remember our relationship to our marriage is an example of our relationship with Christ. Israel dealt treacherously with the Lord so the backslide (divorce) and they left God. God did not want them going after other gods, so He cried out for them to "return" in Jeremiah 3:22.

Since God is married to the backslider, He is committed to warn Israel to return (reconcile).

In Mark 10:1-8 (KJV), *"And he arose from thence, and cometh into the coasts of Judaea by the farther side of Jordan: and the people resort unto him again; and, as he was wont, he taught them again. And the Pharisees came to him, and asked him, Is it lawful for a man to put away his wife? tempting him. And he answered and said unto them, What did Moses command you? And they said, Moses suffered to write a bill of divorcement, and to put her away. And Jesus answered and said unto them, For the hardness of your heart he wrote you this precept. But from the beginning of the creation God made them male and female. For this cause shall a man leave his father and mother, and cleave to his wife; And they twain shall be one flesh: so then they are no more twain, but one flesh."*

In verse two, we see the Pharisees tempting him, asking a question to spurn an answer. Is it lawful for a man to put away his wife? In those times, they were seeking divorce for any and every reason. He replied, "What did Moses command you?" They answered, "Moses suffered to write a bill of divorcement (a legal document)." So, does this contradict that divorce was allowed by God? Jesus answered them, and said, **"For the hardness of your heart he wrote you this percept."** Hardness of heart was a condition (mind) that the people were in—backsliders, hard hearted and rebellious people. Divorce is for this type of people as well as every other sin or doctrine against God.

In verse seven, it gives a man instructions; verse eight, how they shall become; verse nine, God joins the marriage through vows in His presence. From the beginning, divorce was not so and was repaired through Christ.

What therefore God hath joined together; let not man put asunder.

Note: a judge (man or woman) in divorce court is a man putting you asunder!

CHAPTER 8

JEZEBEL SPIRIT; DESTROYER OF COVENANTS

Jezebel is a character who was a Phoenician. She was the wife of Ahab, the king of Northern Israel. Her story is intriguing and full of manipulation, shedding of innocent blood and deception. She introduced the Northern Kingdom of Israel to Baal worship, a pagan God. She was defiant and against the true God and everything He stood for. She waged war against God's prophets and killed many of His prophets who were bearers of that truth. She is known for her manipulation to undo her husband's authority and even had a man land token by deception. Even though Ahab was king, his wife was really ruling, which enters another spirit (the spirit of Ahab), which is more or less a spirit of timidity, co-dependency and less dominant. The spirit of Jezebel is more dominant and controlling although through deceptive means. These two spirits are dominant in covenant relationships. It's almost like a role reversal which goes against God's order for the family. The woman rules over the man; the man is viewed as weak. Jezebel's spirit is also characterized as imprudent, shameless, or morally unrestrained.

"But I have this against you, that you tolerate that woman Jezebel, who calls herself a prophetess and is teaching and seducing my servants to practice sexual

immorality and to eat food sacrificed to idols" (Revelation 2:20 ESV).

The spirit is a spirit of antichrist, self-love and idolatry. Its traits can be found in men but more commonly in women. It all falls under the agenda of what's taking place in today's world with the de-masculinization of men and the masculinity of women. This spirit is often related to a **narcissist**. A narcissist is someone with a mental condition brought on by a tragic event like molestation that lacks empathy. They are grandiose, selfish, manipulators, liars, and act like children. When you enter into a relationship with a person with this spirit, you enter into a soul-tie. A soul-tie is a deep spiritual connection. It's like being hooked together with an invisible cord. Most of the time, you will be in a deep soul-tie with an ultimate agenda to have you submit. Once they have your submission, they put you in a place of safety, safe zone or shelf you. "Why?" you ask. In a narcissist view, they look at you as supply. Supply can be a place to stay, car, money, validation, etc. When they have you in a place of submission, you become a safe supply (guaranteed) to feed their fuel which is attention (validation). To keep you in their safe zone, they employ a lot of tactics which may seem to be very childish but very demonic.

- Mind games - have you constantly doubting yourself, confusion.
- Idealize/discard - give you loads of attention then take away; disappearing acts, disrespect.
- Gaslighting - when they twist the truth; it isn't an all-out lie, but they leave out critical information. All this does is keep you in a sense of bewilderment and confusion to keep you doubting yourself.

- Sexual temptation - use sex to manipulate, to receive a desired outcome.
- Mirror - they mimic your traits and characteristics, so they basically mirror you and you fall in love with your own qualities. A covert narcissist will gain intel on what you like and love and then become that. That's the trap.
- Push/pull - this is to further lower your self-esteem. Give then take, give then take.

The more one goes through this cycle of abuse (because that's what it is), the more addicted and entangled they become. All of this is to enforce their emotional manipulation; you lose self-esteem and confidence and become dependent. That's why many psychiatrists equal the Jezebel spirit to a narcissist. I say anything that affects the mind or plays on the mind is demonic, as this spirit's ultimate goal is to steal, kill and destroy. You will feel like yourself trapped in a black widow's web, with the web being deception.

There are many interesting views and topics on narcissism on the internet from licensed professionals. If you feel like your partner is suffering from this, then please seek help. Sometimes, a person can become a narcissist when they experienced a traumatic experience in their youth like molestation or abuse.

CHAPTER 9

WHAT ABOUT ME?

We see the mounting evidence against popular church doctrine. Even in other scriptures found in the Apocrypha Ecclesiasticus 23:18, which helps make the scriptures harmonize. *"A man that breaketh wedlock, saying thus in his heart, Who seeth me? I am compassed about with darkness, the walls cover me, and nobody seeth me; what need I to fear? the most High will not remember my sins:"*

In verse 23, we see the Most High use direct language to itemize infractions against His covenant. *"For first, she hath disobeyed the law of the most High; and secondly, she hath trespassed against her own husband; and thirdly, she hath played the whore in adultery, and brought children by another man."*

People cannot wrap their head around marriage being for a lifetime. They view it as being forced to be in a relationship under extreme conditions. Cases such as physical abuse, which comes in more than one form. You can have habits which may be detrimental to your spouse and you. It may be, but often times just viewed as the only type, which may be physical. However, I identify bad habits that can affect you physically, i.e., health. I deem that physical abuse also.

We have cases of verbal abuse which is self-explanatory. Constantly belittling someone. We have cases of mental abuse, which I classify as someone hurting you by their actions. We try and self-reason that God is a merciful God and He is. So, we know surely God would not want someone to stay in a situation like this. (What about me, God) is the syndrome. However, if you think I am going to say stay in the relationship like some on the extreme right, you are wrong. To people living under these conditions, God already made a provision. It is the **Law of Separation**. The Lord knew (because He is an all-knowing) that two people in some cases just cannot live together.

*"But and if she depart, let her remain **unmarried** or be **reconciled** to her husband:..."* (1 Corinthians 7:11 KJV). If two people are to depart, the scripture says they are to remain unmarried or be reconciled to our spouse. This speaks to what the Bible clearly teaches and speaks: forgiveness, witness, exalt, and reconciliation. Even if your spouse chooses to backslide and disrespect your union, it does not mean you have to be the same. The Bible commands us to save ourselves. Too many are quick to get into relationships, not to mention they do not believe in waiting for a divorce. It is just not healthy—physically, mentally, or spiritually.

I pose a statement. Many will even feel that this proposition I just explained is unfair. Also, should I be free to love who I want? That is the whole concept of free will, that is the greatest love and demonstration of love. When we choose to love, it is a conscious decision. Love is not simply an emotion or a feeling, but consists of emotions and feelings. Before one can love their spouse, they must learn the love of God, in other words, learn the ways of God. If you are in one of these situations, God understands, but God is also into the reconciliation business, not dissolving. If there is no way to reconcile, we are commanded to remain unmarried as long as your spouse liveth. Would this not be the perfect time to devote oneself to the word of God and master oneself? So, society does not hinder us. Become a better you, find the idolatry in your life, which is the beginning of all sin. Even when it comes to sexual desires, which when committed outside of marriage is an infraction against God's law. One must understand as a disciple of God's law, we are not supposed to be engaging in sex anyway. Sex before marriage is fornication committed by an unmarried person is a fornicator. Even if we fall, we are commanded to repent and that does not mean stay in it, but turn from it. So, even though sexual desires and temptations are real, it is not a justification for divorce and remarriage as long as your spouse remains alive. If they pass away, then it is fine to remarry. A covenant is voided by shedding of blood, death. The sacrifices at the altars in the Old Testaments signify this in reference to Christ's death.

Abuse is another real topic, and you have to ask that question, "Why is my spouse abusive?" Was he or she like that in the beginning? Let's assume they pass the 90-day test. A famous author once said a lady should wait at least 90 days before having sex. This is why relationships have come to the devaluing state that they're in now. A woman is to preserve herself until marriage. I know in the real world it seems outdated and impossible but true. I say 90 days to see what a person is truly like then you proceed from there, but it doesn't mean sex. The highest value a woman has to give away is herself. Now you can begin to troubleshoot from which the abuse steams from.

- Is it a hardened heart?
- Is it from past events?
- Is it the person's character?
- Is it retaliation?

- Is it from drugs or alcohol?
- Is it from hurt?
- Is it a mental condition?

You have to ask yourself these important questions. If it was the character of your spouse to be abusive, did you not see the red flags? Now this is not to imply in any way it was your fault. If the abuse occurred after a traumatic event and they were deeply wounded, then how do we proceed? Your spouse's retaliation with abuse is in itself a problem because abused people have the potential to become abusers. The reason I draw this conclusion, because if reconciliation is to be an end goal, you have to see all in which both parties have done in a totality. If abuse is present, seek professional help.

Case Study:

If a person has divorced their spouse and let's say they remarried. They get along fine and have a beautiful home with kids on top of that. Let's add they weren't even saved in the first marriage but came to Christ in the second. Let's say they even repent, and I will get back to that, the question is: does or will God forgive them? The short answer is yes but only when you repent. See repentance means to turn back from to make a hundred and eighty degree turn from **(if the scriptures say remarriage is permitted when your spouse has died).** So, are they still living in adultery? Yes, because adultery is not a one-time sin. But sexual relations with someone who is not spiritually yours, that's an ongoing sin.

I know a lot of people and I mean a lot who will argue, "But what about the kids?" That man is still responsible to take care of those kids in all his families, but it doesn't make the second marriage legal.

Sexual immorality isn't just fornication and adultery, it's homosexuality (I'm sorry), lust, bestiality, and pornography. So, it's not just the adulterer who must refrain from unlawful sexual actions. A lot more would say it's still insane on rules about how I live my life. But let's just lay in the now, the physical something you can imagine and relate to. Spiritual laws are like gravity; it is there but you can't see it.

If you want to run a business, government, military or any organization (even a sports team), you have to have rules of conduct. You cannot just have everybody doing their own thing, It will not work. Remember, I didn't say diversity. I'm saying conduct; a way of doing things.

This is the attitude of the world: 'everybody wants to do their own thing.' Our ways are more selfish and about attitude, mindset and rebellion. An interesting fact is the divorce rate has been steadily dropping since 1980. So, is our younger generation getting wiser and marrying later and longer? In some cases, this fact is true. However, in most, it speaks to the changing mentality of the people today. You have more people cohabiting instead of marriage on one spectrum. On the other end of that spectrum people are becoming more educated on and making more informed decisions. The decline in the divorce rate is concentrated amongst people with college degrees. For the less educated, the divorce rate is closer to those of the peak 70s.

As marriages are becoming one of the many institutions from which the less educated and poor are excluded, can you imagine somebody dealing with the everyday problems of poverty compounded with the problems of trying to support a family? However, we can't give all the way into this. As Kingdom believers, we know God will provide. We also know believers perish for lack of knowledge.

So, this is my prayer that every broken marriage will be healed. Even in the state of separation or divorce, concentrate on you and your relationship with God.

- Learn and inquire more about God.
- Learn about covenants and marriage.
- Let the scriptures speak to you.
- Learn about you (your temple).
- Learn about soul-ties.
- Learn God's moral compass.

*Who we marry is one of the most important decisions in life one that would influence the level of happiness, growth and success like no other choice - Nathan Workman

*Make your relationship a priority even when you are very busy with life care's. This is vital for a long and happy marriage.

*Fall in love with the process of becoming the very best version of yourself.

*A good marriage isn't something you find; it's something you make and you have to keep on making it.

*Understanding comes when you stand under the knowledge (wisdom) of God - James Stover